MY JOURNEY FROM PRISON HOSTAGE TO LEADERSHIP EXECUTIVE

How My Journey From Prison Hostage to Leadership Executive
5 Important Keys to Becoming an Extraordinary Leader

Donnie Houston, M.Ed.

Published by Game Changer Publishing

ISBN: 978-1-7365491-3-1

www.PublishABestSellingBook.com

DEDICATION

This book is dedicated to my parents, Johnny and Mary Houston. Although you are not here on earth, the lessons and values you taught me I continue to use as guiding principles for my life's purpose and direction.

To my wonderful wife, Karen - When God made you, he knew I would need a life partner who is strong, God-fearing, and possesses unshakeable strength to deal with the ups and downs of life. I am forever grateful and blessed to have you as my friend, wife, and life partner.

DOWNLOAD YOUR FREE GIFTS

Read This First

Just to say thanks for buying and reading my book, I would like to give you a free bonus gift 100% FREE, no strings attached!

To Download Now, Visit:
www.DonnieHoustonSpeaks.com/Freegift

MY JOURNEY FROM PRISON HOSTAGE TO LEADERSHIP EXECUTIVE

5 Important Keys to Becoming an Extraordinary Leader

Donnie Houston, M.Ed.

www.PublishABestSellingBook.com

FOREWORD

WITH THE UNFORTUNATE MANIFESTATION of Covid-19, the economy has changed the way we work and how leaders lead. There has been so much discussion of the importance of leadership and what makes a great leader. Donnie felt this was the right time to add his voice to the leadership conversation, thus the reason for this book.

This book is a great read for leaders on every level and provides practical principles to re-energize, inspire, and improve efficiency within an organization. It gives young leaders things to consider before taking the leadership plunge!

Donnie is a seasoned leader who has marshaled the respect from his direct reports, superiors, and powerbrokers in the senior housing industry. As his wife, I had the opportunity to have a courtside seat to watch Donnie's maturation as a husband, father, leader, and man of God. This book is the result of years of study, hard work, successes, and failures that will help all who read it improve their leadership skills and interpersonal relationships. Our wish is to stir up the gift inside of you to help you become more, to dream more, and for you to ultimately move from being ordinary to an extraordinary leader! Enjoy!

~ Karen D. Houston

Table of Contents

INTRODUCTION

MY NAME IS DONNIE HOUSTON. I am a 59-year-old man with an incredible story to share that will stir up the gift inside of you and challenge you to go from ordinary to extraordinary.

Twenty-plus years ago, my life changed forever when I was taken hostage while working at the MCC Correctional Center in San Diego, CA. The takeover happened so fast, and with such precision, the only thing I could think about is how to survive.

The odds of survival were not in my favor. Both inmates who held me captive were in their early thirties and were sentenced to life in prison. In fact, the leader Ernesto Cruz was serving a double life sentence! My ability to negotiate my release was nonexistent. In fact, in the prison culture, inmates got "strips" or "street credit" for assaulting and killing correctional personnel. Imagine being held hostage for 17 hours by two inmates who had several killings on their resume! My life hung in the balance with every tick of the clock.

During the next seventeen hours, I was assaulted beyond your imagination. It was during this time of terror that I recalled the words of my dear mother, "If you ever get in trouble, recite Psalm 23." The Lord spoke to me in a calm voice with a question, *Are you ready to go?* I said, "No."

The Lord continued, *I am going to get you out of here, but it will take a minute. You will not be harmed or injured. Oh, and you know your wife wants to have a baby.*

My response was, "I know, but I am living on the fringes now. How will I provide?"

The Lord said, *If I can get you out of this, I can do anything? Do not worry, I will provide.*

17 hours later, the FBI and SWAT stormed the cell, and I was free from my captors. I was tortured and stabbed, but as the Lord promised, I was not injured! In fact, if you look at my chest today, there are no visible marks of the stabbing. Praise God!

Now the real work started as I attempted to repair my life after such a horrific life-threatening event. After many sessions with the psychologist, I was diagnosed with a severe case of PTSD. My prognosis was I would never return to meaningful work again, and I felt as if my ability to be a contributing member of society had been taken from me. I attended a meeting with one of the correctional administrator power brokers and was offered total disability.

Accepting such an offer would have afforded me a safe and comfortable life, but the contributions to society I wanted to make, my dreams, and my legacy were not for sale. I refuse to succumb to the fear of playing it safe, I am now living a life of self-actualization, and I want to share with you principles that will help you move from ordinary to exceptional.

CHAPTER 1

"I'M GOING TO give you a break, Houston."

"I'm going to let you decide how you want to die."

It was a choice I never imagined I'd have to make six hours earlier. It was 9 p.m. and just another December night with the Metropolitan Correctional Center inmates in downtown San Diego. I'd been a prison guard there for a couple of years, a twenty-nine-year-old man who left a stable but stagnant job with the state of Michigan in my hometown of Muskegon, to find a career with more opportunity for advancement in Southern California. My then-girlfriend, Karen, followed me west, and we'd just been married in June. We had plans to build our life together, have a family, and my work as a prison guard was intended to provide the finances and the stability to make that a reality.

Earlier that night, right before she dropped me off at the prison, Karen shared her ongoing concern for my safety. It was understandable, of course, but it was becoming a persistent worry for her, and I again tried to reassure her. After all, the high-rise detention facility was one of the top federal prisons in the country. It hadn't had a single hostage situation in the 15 years since it opened in 1974. I was trained. I was confident. And I wasn't afraid.

That night, when another guard and I approached the cell block in the high-security area on the fifth floor, we had no reason to fear. It was specially designed to restrict the movement of the prisoners. Only one block was allowed out at a time, and the area that the inmates were released into for recreation periods was small. The set up was as secure as it possibly could be, but you never know what will happen when you're dealing with desperate men in a desperate situation.

We approached the main, barred gate entering into the cell block. Fluorescent lights bathed the common area with their harsh glow. Rows of cells were on each side of us, not barred cages as you might expect, but each was a cinder block room with a solitary steel door at the front. The door had a narrow, vertical window on the top half, just above a slot where inmates received their meals, mail, or any other items they were allowed to have. Usually, I'd stay behind the gate, let my colleague open it, go inside the common area alone, and open the cells. However, I knew one of the men in the first cell, Emilio Bravo, was a nasty, tricky guy who had it in for my fellow guard. I didn't know why Bravo had the grudge, but I felt it was safest to follow my partner into the common area as an unspoken deterrent to Bravo against trying anything funny.

My colleague took his key and unlocked Bravo's cell door. I heard the *pop* of the lock release and then watched the door fly open.

As Bravo burst out, I moved myself between him and the other guard. My first priority was to protect my fellow worker.

Bravo moved right up into my face, and I backed away slightly, saying. "I don't want no problems, Bravo. You the man, alright? I don't want no problems."

He rushed me, and we started grappling. At the same time, Bravo's cellmate, Jose Rodriguez, must've come out as well, presumably to go after my colleague. But the next thing I knew, the other guard was gone, and Rodriguez was behind me. A sharp point was pressed against the small of my back next to my spine.

"Don't move!" Rodriguez yelled as Bravo increased his grip on me. I didn't say anything. I was unable to fight with a shank at my back. I knew I was in trouble.

Quickly, they guided me into the cell, and I saw they had already ripped their bedspread into strips suitable for tying up my hands and feet. I heard the cell door slam behind me and then, to my surprise, heard it lock from the outside. I looked toward the narrow window. In the commotion, another guard, different from the one I was with before, had come into the common area and locked the door before he realized I was inside the cell with the two inmates. Seeing his mistake, he started to unlock the door, I assume, to attempt to rescue me.

"No!" Bravo screamed. "If anyone comes into this cell, I'll kill him!"

I was shoved to the floor and forced to lie on my stomach. As they were tying my feet crosswise and my hands behind my back, I swiveled my torso to get a glimpse of the two men in their zippered orange jumpsuits. Both had their dark hair slicked back. Bravo had a coarse salt-and-pepper beard and, at five-foot-ten, was smaller than me. Rodriguez was bigger than I was, but it was clear Bravo was calling the shots in this altercation. That wasn't surprising - I understood Bravo to be a bad, bad man, capable of anything. I already knew that Bravo was apparently a Satan worshipper because of the huge deal he made months earlier about his religious rights being violated if he wasn't allowed to have a Satanic bible and other related materials in his cell.

When they finished binding me, Bravo sat on the floor to my left, took the shank, and pressed it, just a little, into my lower back. I winced and gritted my teeth.

"Every time, I'm going to go deeper and deeper," he said, and moments later, he did. I rocked back and forth with each stab in an attempt to alleviate the depth of the wounds. Bravo was obviously skilled with the shank. He never drove it too deep but just enough to cause searing pain with each penetration. He was slow... Methodical... Precise.

Unfortunately, my torture was just beginning.

After about ten minutes of this abuse, Bravo pulled me into a sitting position and dragged me to the corner of the cell. I rested my back against the cold, grey wall. Both men looked to the door as confused activity continued outside. Rodriguez looked at me.

"There are guys out there in black, ninja suits," he said.

"That must be SWAT or the FBI," I said quietly.

"You'll be dead by the time they get to you," Bravo added.

He approached me, bent down, took me by the collar, and punched me in my left eye again and again. I tried to anticipate the blows and turn my head to the right to lessen the impact of each, but Bravo's strikes did their damage. It wasn't long before my vision was obscured, but with my right eye, I saw someone had shoved a landline phone into the door slot. Bravo pulled it in toward me, took the receiver, and repeatedly hit me with it on the side of the head. The hard plastic shell of the phone receiver thudded against my temple, my ear, and my skull. Somehow, I remained conscious through it all. After a while, Bravo stopped and held the receiver out to me.

"Are you married?" he asked.

I was dizzy and in a haze of pain. I thought it best not to risk a lie. "Yes."

"Call her!" he growled.

Of course, I was badly injured and couldn't dial, so I told him the number. He handed me the receiver. Even in my woozy state, I knew that by then, the prison authorities would've notified Karen about the situation and that she'd already have left home, making her way back to the prison. When the answering machine picked up, I told Bravo, and he snatched the phone from me.

"I'm going to kill your husband!" he shouted, adding several curses before slamming the receiver down on the cradle.

I knew what he was doing. Everything was designed to make me afraid and reduce my resolve. It was everything I could do to keep his tactics from working.

Over the next few hours, I was randomly hit and kicked. Most of the abuse was inflicted by Bravo. Rodriguez rarely hit me and hardly spoke. Bravo paced and cursed, fussed, and raged. He was on the phone periodically with a hostage negotiator. His demands were numerous. He wanted keys to the cell door, a shotgun, access to the media, and a helicopter ready to return him and Rodriguez to Cuba. He wanted me to go on the air with the media and talk about alleged misdeeds he'd experienced in prison with the clergy. Sometimes, he settled down long enough to show me newspaper clippings detailing, he said, the stories of people he'd killed that the police didn't know anything about. He was raving, there was no doubt, but in a way, I was glad. It was redirecting him away from abusing me further—or worse.

After a while, Bravo announced that he was going to kill me at three o'clock. I don't know why that time was chosen, but as it approached, he started giving me a countdown.

"One a-m... Two a-m." he chanted.

At one point, he took the shank, the smaller of two that I observed in the cell, and traced an X in the air right above my uniform in places where he said he was going to stab me. Over my jugular. My spine. My heart. Sometimes, he pulled his hand back and then launched the shank toward the spot, diverting at the last second so that it didn't touch me but slashed past me into the wall making the metal sound *"chink"* against concrete. Again, he was practiced at the torture. I was convinced he'd done it several times before on the outside to those who went against him.

Finally, the time came. "Houston, it's 2:55. I'm getting ready to kill you. Do you have any last words? Anything at all?"

I was succinct. "Don't kill me."

He looked upward, like he was suddenly pondering something, and smiled. "I'm going to give you a break, Houston."

Hope leaped within. *Maybe this fool isn't going to kill me after all,* I thought.

And then Bravo hissed, "I'm going to let you decide how you want to die."

My adrenaline surged. My shoulders slumped. He directed my blurred vision to the floor. I saw some pills on the ground with powder around them. I hadn't noticed either one until this moment.

Bravo continued, "You can take these pills and have convulsions until you die. Or I can stab you anywhere you want as many times as you'd like until you die. Or I'm going to hang you. Either way, my god, Satan, has told me to kill you."

When Bravo said that, fear, pure and unabated, washed over me. Then an image of my mother's face, misty in the cobwebs of my mind, came to me, and I heard her say what she'd always told me as a boy.

"Donnie, when you get in trouble, say the twenty-third Psalm."

As a teenager, I'd read that Psalm and other passages from the Bible to Mama at night. She was illiterate, and I knew she was comforted by hearing scripture before she went to sleep.

Well, Mama, I thought, *I'm sure in trouble right now. I guess this is as good a time as any to pull it out.* So I started reciting silently in my head the words I'd spoken so often all those years ago.

The Lord is my shepherd; I shall not want.

He makes me to lie down in green pastures:
He leads me beside the still waters.

He restores my soul:
He leads me in the paths of righteousness for His name's sake.

Yea, though I walk through the valley of the shadow of death,
I will fear no evil;
For You are with me;
Your rod and Your staff, they comfort me.

You prepare a table before me in the presence of my enemies;
You anoint my head with oil;
My cup runs over.

Surely goodness and mercy shall follow me
All the days of my life;
And I will dwell in the house of the Lord
Forever.

(Psalm 23:1-6 New King James Version)

After I thought the words to myself, I neither experienced a sense of peace nor one of increased dread. Nothing really changed at all—except that my brain then started reeling through my subconscious, like a grainy old home movie shown on a projector screen, events from my life, one after another. There I was, sitting on the floor in my first-grade classroom, the smell of paste sweet in the air as Miss Armstrong sat in the middle of the circle of children and taught us spelling words. Then I was in the neighborhood where I grew up, looking from the porch of my house and beyond the front yard to see Mr. Mack, the leg amputee who lived across the street. As a teen, I went to the store for him or trod down into his basement to carry up his laundry. Then I heard Miss Lindsay, my godmother, hollering at me from next door as I arrived home from high school with my buddies.

"Now Donnie, you know your Mama don't want you to have no boys over right now, don't ya?"

"Yeah, I know," I said, "and I've only got an hour before she gets home."

Then I was in the driver's seat of the old brown, four-door Ford Custom that Daddy bought for me—my first car as a young adult. I pumped my arms as I turned the corner minus power steering and the AM radio blaring Donna Summer.

I thought about the children I fathered before I met Karen and how they were going to react when they found out I was dead.

I thought of my new bride, our newlywed bliss, and what she was going to do without me.

Is this how my life is going to end? Is this it? I thought.

Then another voice spoke. "I'm gonna get you out of here, and you are going to be okay. You aren't going to be crazy. Nothing is going to happen to you. But it's going to be a while. You're gonna have to sit tight."

My mind whirled. A fourth person had not entered the cell. I didn't know where the voice was coming from, but it was just as clear and real as though we were sitting across the table from each other having a conversation over coffee.

"When I get you out of here, you know Karen is gonna want to have a baby."

It was a statement, not a question. Mentally, I responded—and it was the strangest retort, given the circumstances of the moment.

I'm still paying child support! How can I take care of another baby?

"Well, if I can get you out of this, I can do anything, can't I? Don't worry. I'll provide."

"Okay." This time, I said it aloud.

Bravo looked at me and yelled, "Who the hell are you talkin' to?"

CHAPTER 2

THE HOUSTON FAMILY WAS brought up in church. Not going was never an option. I was there with Mama, Daddy, and my four sisters and two brothers every time the door was open at New Mt. Zion Missionary Baptist Church.

That's all it ever was for me, really—a place I had to be. But that doesn't mean I didn't like it. It was an essential part of our lives. Daddy was a deacon; Mama was on the mothers' board; my siblings were ushers or in the choir, and I played the drums. We went to Sunday school, worship service, and we were back again for every revival meeting, but I never had a born-again experience. I never really talked to God as a youngster, and I don't recall Him ever talking to me.

Muskegon Heights was a predominantly black, working-class, inner-city neighborhood whose uniform grid of streets was lined by one- or two-story houses with pitched roofs and covered porches sandwiched grassy front and back yards, shaded by tall fir and spruce trees. High in crime and poverty today, Muskegon Heights sure didn't seem that way back when I was growing up there in the 70s. It was safe and filled with families. My parents were hard-working, honest, God-fearing people who provided a wholesome, nurturing environment for us after moving there from Louisiana before I was born.

Daddy worked first shift at a piston ring factory until a back injury forced him to leave that job. Around that same time, Mama became sick with what I don't remember exactly because I was small then. She spent so much time in the hospital that I recall a family friend, Miss Margaret, telling my Daddy that if Mama were to pass, she would be glad to take my sister, Sheila, and me into her care. We were the youngest of the siblings—my eldest sister was twenty-two years older than me. Every one of my brothers and sisters had a role to play. My second oldest sister, also named Margaret, was like a second mother. John was my protector who took care of any of the bullies, and Ralph, who went on to play for a while in the National Basketball Association, was the one I most wanted to be like. I was closest to Sheila because we were only four years apart in age, but we all got along, and we all loved our parents.

Eventually, Mama fought her way back to health and worked jobs as a housekeeper and at the celery plant while Daddy opened up a convenience store in the projects, worked part-time at a funeral home, and drove a snowplow in the winter until the injury settlement from the factory provided a little financial breathing room. At one point, Mama opened up a charge account for me at a clothes store called

Mister Brother Man, which was owned by a friend. She'd send me over after calling ahead.

"I'm sending Donnie Boy over. Now, make sure that whatever he gets he can wear to church."

I had more than most kids in my neighborhood, and I never lacked for anything. Well, except for good grades. Try as I might, I was a lousy student. I got Cs and Ds from elementary through high school, and despite reading scripture to Mama as a teen, I didn't do a whole lot with books outside of that. I was more interested in hanging out with the guys, chasing girls when I got old enough, and playing basketball. Like most inner-city kids, I dreamed of playing in the NBA and always got a place on the court with the older boys, even if it was only by reputation.

"Hey, that's Big Ralph's brother," they said when I arrived. "He can play with us."

I was a decent player—good enough to later earn an athletic scholarship. But first, my academic pursuits—well, more correctly stated, Mama's academic pursuits for me—took me all the way west to Arizona right after I graduated high school in 1979. She sent me there to live with my brother, Ralph, by then married and done with his professional basketball career, to go to school at Mesa Community College in the Phoenix metropolitan area. I arrived in June, my first time ever outside the state of Michigan, and immediately noticed two things. First, it was hot—darn hot. Second, it was multicultural. There were whites, Mexicans, Apaches, and even interracial couples on campus. I wasn't ready for the culture shock, but even worse was the fact that I wasn't ready to go to college. School started in August, and I made it until the end of September. Since I considered myself to be something of a fashion plate, I took a class in fashion merchandising—but I didn't know what that was. I was the only guy in the room. A teacher in a morning class gave me three chapters of reading homework, and then the same thing happened in another class in the afternoon. It was too much. I was utterly unprepared academically and socially.

When Mama and Daddy sent me some money to buy a used car, I took it and bought a plane ticket back home. When I arrived, I saw my pastor at the airport.

"You want a ride home, Donnie?" he asked.

I sure did because I hadn't told my parents I was coming. All Mama could say when I arrived was, "Whatcha' doin' here?"

She was disappointed but undeterred. She made me try school again, this time on that basketball scholarship to Grand Rapids Community College, but I again only managed to get through a few months before dropping out. After working some odd jobs, I went back a final time and made it through an entire semester, getting the minimum grade point average required for an athlete.

"How did you ever make it this far?" one English teacher asked.

It was a valid question. I had no idea, and I didn't go any further than that. It took too much out of me. School wore me out.

It was then, after a few more part-time jobs, that I landed a position with benefits at the Muskegon Regional Center with the State of Michigan. It wasn't much, but it was enough to let me keep my own place, a one-bedroom apartment downtown. By then, I'd fathered my children and was paying child support for them. I got along fine with their mothers. In neither case was I in love with these ladies, nor did we get married. But I fulfilled my responsibilities toward them as best as I could—it was a trait ingrained in me by my Daddy.

After starting at the regional center in 1983, I met Karen Hilliard at a gathering of friends at Lake Michigan. We hit it off immediately, and our first date was at a little Chinese place on 28th Street. We dated more, sometimes just hanging out at each other's apartments. The relationship got pretty serious pretty quick, and from my perspective, it was easy to understand why. Karen was kind. She not only understood that I had an obligation to my children, but she embraced and respected it.

"I know that what you did wasn't right," she told me, "but there's a lot of guys who just run from their responsibilities. You've taken them on."

That affirmed me as a young man. Karen cared for my children and me (to this day, they call her "mother"). More than that, I felt she was a person who could stand the rain—she was strong, with a positive personality and attitude about the realities of life. For the next six months, we enjoyed the good company of others, and we reveled in time spent with each other because we had so much in common. I knew our relationship could go somewhere significant—and that was the catalyst to look beyond my job at the regional center and see if I could achieve something better.

But that was going to involve taking a risk. By then, Ralph and his family had moved to Chula Vista, California, in the San Diego area, where he had a great job and a nice two-story townhouse. I called him up.

"I'm thinking about coming out to California. I want to try to get a fresh start in my career and find a job where I can move up. I don't have any prospects yet, but I believe I can find something out there with a future," I said. "Could I stay with you until I get on my feet?"

"Sure, Donnie," he said. "We'd love to have you."

I added, "I'd like to bring my girlfriend with me."

He didn't hesitate. He, too, knew that Karen was special. "I was hoping you would. We'll be waiting for you guys."

That afternoon, I went to see Karen at her apartment. We sat side-by-side on the steps in front of her duplex. It was near the end of a hot and humid day, and I mopped a trickle of sweat off of my brow. My mood matched the sticky weather. I was nervous—and steeled myself to hear her say, "Hey, it's been real, but good luck. Go ahead and go."

I leaned in close and told her about my desire to leave the regional center and why I felt I needed the change. I told her I didn't have another job to go to yet and reminded her about Ralph and where he lived.

"I'm moving to California—and I'd like you to come with me."

She smiled the same way I'd seen her smile when I cracked a silly joke. "Yeah, I'll come."

I let out a huge breath and felt a lightness in my chest. "You will?"

"Oh yeah!"

I put both arms around her shoulders and hugged her tight. "I think this is going to be a fresh start for both of us. I'm leaving in two weeks."

"I'll be out there within the month," she said.

In that moment, I knew that our expressions of "I love you" were far more than words—they were a commitment to one another. She was going to share in my risk and my hopes for a better future. We were going to do it together.

Karen and I stayed in the guest room of his townhouse for about three months. I found a full-time job at a privately owned facility for the mentally and physically disabled as an attendant, work that was similar to what I had been doing back in Michigan. I knew that it wasn't where I wanted to end up, but it allowed us to find our legs. Karen worked part-time for Ralph at his employer, and we eventually had the money to get our own place, a two-bedroom, one-bath apartment in a low rent district. It was so close to the highway that we had to keep the sliding glass door to the balcony closed just to hear ourselves think, much less have a conversation. The place had its oddities. The water in the toilet was scalding hot, leaving condensation on our butts every time we went to the bathroom. Karen once got trapped *inside* the apartment because the locking mechanisms on the front and sliding doors were so funky. It was not uncommon to go out to the car only to have an illegal immigrant from across the nearby Mexican border roll out from beneath the vehicle where he'd taken shelter for the night. But we didn't care. It was home—our home.

One evening, I was once again pouring through the newspaper want ads when I saw a full-page advertisement about becoming a guard with the Federal Department of Corrections. They were hiring with no previous experience or college degree required. It promised opportunities for advancement and good benefits. It was perfect. In short order, I applied, was interviewed, and hired. I was assigned to work under an experienced guard at the Metropolitan Correctional Center and started going through my paces doing less hazardous duties. After a couple of months, I was sent out to the Federal Law Enforcement Training Center in Glynco, Georgia. Academy training lasted four weeks and consisted of everything from learning vital administrative tasks to firearms training, how to search a cell, hand-to-hand combat—and what to do in case you were ever taken hostage. One day we were in the classroom when all of a sudden, a bunch of guys with automatic weapons burst into the room. The lights went off, and to my surprise, some people around me started screaming.

C'mon, man, I thought. *This is the safest place in America. This is obviously a drill.*

I stayed cool and played along through the exercise. The instructor taught three basic rules for being a hostage. First, never try to escape unless you are certain that you can get away. Second, don't try to fight back and be a hero—that stuff's only on television. Third, they said you gotta relax and understand one thing—you're going to be there for a while. Surviving as a hostage is an act of endurance that's more of a mental game than anything else.

I enjoyed the training at Glynco and returned home confident but with a renewed perspective that a prison could be taken over at any time. It is a place and a profession that deserves your respect and requires your reverence and attention. My roles at Metropolitan gradually increased, and I even took part in a special tour of duty back at Glynco, helping to guard a group of prisoners from Philadelphia who were being housed there temporarily while their facility back in Pennsylvania was rebuilt after a fire. During that tour, I sent all of the extra pay I earned to Karen, and she used it to help us catch up on delinquent utility bills and to start paying off credit card debt. Shortly after my return, we got a nicer apartment in a better neighborhood. She got a full-time position as an administrative secretary at the University of California, San Diego.

Oh, and we got married, too—but it was not after a get-down-on-your-knees-and-propose sort of engagement. There really wasn't any engagement at all.

"My friend knows a place where we can get married," Karen announced one evening after work.

"Okay," I responded. "You set it all up, and I'll be there."

With that, she made a Saturday appointment for us at the Wedding Bell Chapel, a small, rustic sort of place in a historic area of downtown. Ralph and his wife, Jackie, joined with mutual friends, Terry and Pam Jones (I worked with Terry at the prison, Karen with Pam at the university) to be our sole witnesses at the ceremony. There was a platform with bouquets of flowers on each side. The wedding march was played on a cassette deck by the person who conducted the ceremony, and traditional vows were used with nothing special said by either one of us other than the essential "I do's." She wore an off-the-rack wedding dress, and I had on a double-breasted suit and tie. As we walked outside afterward to pose for some photos, the street was filled with parade-goers for gay-lesbian pride led by the motorcycle group, Dykes on Bikes. It was a quirky addition to the memorable day. We left the chapel as a group and stopped to pick up a fifth of Hennessey and a bucket of chicken on the way back to Ralph's place to celebrate. I only had a sip of the cognac because I had to go to work that night, and I took a few pieces of chicken with me to eat on break.

Getting married to Karen was the most natural thing in the world to do. We loved each other and had become inseparable soul mates— 'til death do us part.

~

Bravo glared at me and raised his fist as if to administer another blow. "I said, who in the hell are you talkin' to?"

I looked up at my captor. "Nobody."

I knew Who I had talked to, of course, but I didn't want to ruffle Bravo at this point. If I was going to take the pills, take the shank, or hang, I wasn't going to choose for him. In fact, I was determined I wasn't going to say anything else at all.

I didn't have to.

Five minutes passed. 10. Then 20. Then an hour. Bravo fussed and fumed, but not once did the subject of the time or manner in which I was going to die come up again. He threatened to kill me, sure, several times—that was no different than anything he'd said in the first six hours of this ordeal. But it was as though the specific directive he'd received from his god, Satan, was now null and void. Really, it was as though he'd never said it in the first place.

I recalled again what the *Voice* told me. "Nothing is going to happen to you. But it's going to be a while."

So I settled back in and relied on a combination of my trust in that *voice* and an application of my hostage training from Glynco to see me through. As a hostage, you move from one crisis to the next.

I'm still alive. That's good, I thought, *but I have to be ready for whatever is going to come next.*

Every now and then, Bravo punched me or kicked me almost, it seemed, out of boredom. He occasionally checked my hands to make sure I wasn't trying to get loose, and that thought did cross my mind several times, but each time, I had to play it through to the end. If I did get loose, grab for one or both of the shanks and missed, what was next?—Surely my death. I started to get claustrophobic, slouched in my little corner of the cell, and my muscles screamed in agony from being tied up. Yet I knew I needed to block all of that out of my mind, or else I'd literally go crazy.

As Bravo engaged in a phone conversation with the FBI SWAT negotiator, I knew their strategy was to drag out the situation to make Bravo and Rodriguez wear down and give up. After all, they couldn't stay awake and aware forever. They had to sleep, and they had to eat. I dozed when I could, more to relax myself than giving in to the drowsiness, and around seven o'clock or so, I asked for something to eat.

Bravo was incredulous. "We're fixin' to kill you, and you're worried about something to eat?"

"Well, I'm hungry, man. Can I get some food?"

Bravo consented, and when the food came, he planned to eat some of it too but had me taste it first, presumably to make sure it wasn't poisoned. I ate very little of the food, but my bladder demanded attention, so I asked if I could urinate. Again, Bravo allowed this and untied my hands and feet so I could straddle the commode and perform the act—but he insisted on holding the shank against the back of my testicles while I stood.

"C'mon, Houston!" Bravo yelled after a minute of standing. "Piss already!"

But I couldn't, not with his blade strategically placed as it was. After another few seconds, I gave up, pulled up my pants, and allowed him to tie me back up. At least I'd managed to stretch my weary muscles.

As morning dawned and Bravo's irritated antics increased, I willed myself to mental vigilance. I couldn't focus on his claims of how many people he'd killed in the past or how many times he abused me physically. I was determined not to show any fear. I also knew that I couldn't allow my mind to think about Karen or the children or my family. There was no going to my happy place or some pretend island paradise. To entertain such thoughts was the first step to insanity.

Staying calm and in the moment was the only weapon I had.

By mid-morning, I noticed that Rodriguez and Bravo were losing their battle with their body clocks. Their eyes and body language betrayed their fatigue. This made them even more on edge. I also journeyed into Bravo's mindset and made some logical and frightening assumptions. First, he realized by now that he wasn't going to get what he wanted. There weren't going to be any keys given to him, no shotgun, no access to the media, and no helicopter to Cuba. He'd kept me alive because I was his leverage, the bargaining chip—and now he surely knew that even if he did kill me, it wasn't going to change anything. He was already serving two natural life sentences, meaning that he could live until a ripe old age, die, come back to life, live it all over again, die again, and still be behind bars. But that didn't mean I was out of danger. On the contrary, Bravo now had another compelling reason to end my life—prison cred. Killing a guard meant stripes in the penitentiary; a lifetime badge of honor; a weapon of fear he could wield even if he ended up at the so-called Alcatraz of the Rockies, the supermax underground prison in Colorado.

Several more hours passed, and as I tried to think what Bravo was thinking, it allowed me to coldly and logically assess my situation. It didn't look good.

"I'm gonna get you out of here," the *Voice* echoed, "and you are going to be okay."

"This wasn't even for you, Houston!" Bravo's booming voice interrupted my reverie. He was up on the top bunk and was seething. "This was for the other guy. He was the one we wanted!"

"Hey, I'll go get him," I told him with as much bravado as I could muster. "It's no problem with me. Just let me go, and I'll bring him to you."

It was a desperate ploy, I knew. But I was starting to think I had nothing to lose.

"You won't come back," Bravo said. "I know that. But now you're here, so I guess I'm gonna have to kill you. What are they gonna do to me anyway? Give me another life? I'm already serving two. What can they do to me?"

Hopelessness seeped in. *He has no skin in this game,* I realized. *Stay calm, man. Remember the Voice. Karen's going to have a baby and—No! Don't think of Karen. Be in the moment. Keep it together.*

But I was starting to fall apart. The strain, the hours, the beatings, the deprivation—it was getting to me. I looked at Bravo and saw nothing but darkness. It was as though the dark hood of the reaper had settled over his head, and the sickle was pointed directly at me.

Bravo jumped down. He had a pillowcase in his hand.

"Houston? I'm hungry. I'm tired. And I'm getting ready to kill you."

He shoved the pillowcase over my head. I smelled my sour breath as I involuntarily gasped for air. I lost it and started screaming.

"Please! Don't kill me!" I pleaded. "I've got a family at home—please!"

I wept and was rocking in place, and I felt the cloth tighten around my neck. The taste of bile filled my throat. Then I heard a slight sound of movement from just outside the cell door. Bravo must've, too—he ripped the pillowcase off of my head.

BOOM! BOOM!

Flashbang stun grenades pierced the airwaves. I looked at Rodriguez, then at the door still unmoving, and then at Bravo. The foot-long shank was in his hand, and he was lowering himself over me. He spoke.

"Let's kill this nigger."

CHAPTER 3

BRAVO CROUCHED OVER ME and then leaned the weight of his body into me. I felt my back press into the concrete wall, its unforgiving mass offering no escape from what was to come. I whimpered, and tears stung my eyes as I looked at the blade and saw Bravo shove it forward to pierce into the center of my chest. Cut through bone and sinew. Puncture my lung or heart.

Yet the sharp pain of incision didn't come. Instead, I felt a thudding punch—*press, grind, press, grind*—as the steel struck my body. But there was no prick or puncture. I didn't know why.

Bravo's expression was one of anger, tinged with surprise. *Grrrrr!* As he growled, he thrust his arm forward, twisted his wrist, and sloped himself into my chest with crushing force. I slid down the wall and away to the left in a vain attempt to reduce the force of his attack. I lay flat on my back, he straddled me and ground the weapon into me as though he were milling stone into pulverized powder.

The shank did not penetrate my flesh.

CRASH! The cell door burst open. Footsteps pounded and shouts reverberated through the chamber. I turned my head to see several pairs of booted feet converge around Rodriguez and then felt Bravo release the pressure on my chest. I saw the shank fall in front of my face, its bounce and clang on the floor announcing its sudden uselessness as a tool of death. I looked upward to see three men grab Bravo and wrestle him away from me.

My brain told me to lift myself up, but the command was ignored as darkness took me.

I slowly opened my eyes only to squint at the bright sunlight. Through the glare, I spied two paramedics on each side of me, engulfed by others with video cameras and microphones. I was on my back and on a bed, plunging forward feet first. I raised my head up just enough to see the ambulance, its back doors opened, but my range of vision was obscured by the oxygen mask on my face.

I laid my head back and peered straight up into the baby blue sky. I was outside. My view spun as the gurney was turned, and then it was rocked as I was lifted and inserted backward and headfirst into the vehicle. The paramedics climbed in with me, and the cacophony of voices outside was muffled as the sterile beeps of life support medical equipment pinged their presence.

I spoke. My voice was gruff, hardly recognizable as my own.

"Karen. I want to see Karen."

Right then, footfalls thumped the floor of the compartment. As though cued from off stage, Karen appeared to my left. The paramedic moved to give her room.

"I'm here, Donnie. I'm right here."

I lifted my arms, saw the IV tube in one of them, and reached both of my hands toward her. They trembled as they enveloped her face, one for each beautiful cheek wet from tears. My fingers traced the paths of their flow, lingering over every precious touch.

"I didn't think I'd ever see you again," I said

"Shhh," she responded. "Just stay quiet, baby. Everything's gonna be okay."

I saw her wince as her eyes darted back and forth, examining my damaged eye and face. Now that I was on the way to the hospital and the shock of being rescued was starting to wear off, I took more notice of the aches and pains from my abuse. They didn't feel as bad as I thought they would. I again wondered why the shank hadn't gone into my chest. *It made no sense*, I thought. *Bravo was a strong man. He knew how to kill.* But somehow, someway, I wasn't impaled.

I stayed awake the entire time I was being examined at the ER at the University of California, San Diego Medical Center. The doctors were in awe that I was alive at all—they and many others had been watching my ordeal play out on the TV news.

"We didn't think you were going to make it," one nurse said with gratitude in her voice.

The doctor and his team tended to my bruises and checked my heart and chest to make sure I was stable and confirmed that there was no mark of any kind on my chest to indicate a stab wound. I was sent home after only two hours, and a *Los Angeles Times* article later quoted a hospital spokesman as saying I had "seemingly no injuries at all."

I'd not put it quite that way, in that, I did eventually need a cornea transplant and still have horrible vision to this day. But it was amazing that my physical injuries were as minor as they were.

Karen drove us home, and when I got out of the car and approached the apartment, I fell to my hands and knees and lowered my face toward the ground. The grass smelled clean, almost like it was freshly cut, and I felt the cool brushstrokes as I rubbed my cheek against the blades. Considering that I have allergies, it was a crazy gesture, and Karen looked at me like I was insane. I got up and went inside and leaned against the wall of the living room to feel the texture of the spackling and the smoothness of the paint. Maybe I was insane, but I reveled in using senses I thought I'd never get to experience again.

I was utterly thrilled simply to be alive.

That afternoon and into the evening, I fielded phone calls from my parents, relatives, and friends, all wishing me well and many saying they had been praying for me. By the end of the telephonic flurry, I was exhausted, but the communications were comforting. That night, both Karen and I got some sleep. That first night and on through to the second and third, everything was okay. We rested sufficiently and slept well—and while I knew God had intervened in that prison cell, I didn't understand it. He saved me and apparently had a purpose for me, but I didn't yet know why.

But I did learn that the *Voice* kept its word. On the fourth day, Karen announced that she was indeed pregnant. The due date was in August. I was thrilled, but the first chance I was alone, I quietly and somewhat fearfully talked to the *Voice*.

I thought that was going to be down the road a bit, I nervously declared. *I'm not sure I'm ready for this. Not right now. Why does it have to be now?*

No response. The *Voice* exercised its right to remain silent.

It was unfortunate because that's when it started—the sudden and shocking appearance of other wounds, deeper and far worse than anything physical.

I was awakened by the sound of glass shattering and wood splintering. I jolted straight up in the bed and knew exactly what was happening. I flipped off the covers and stood up.

"I know you're out there!" I yelled.

Karen raised up from her resting place on the far side of the bed.

"Donnie?" Her voice was alert, though still groggy. "What is it?"

"Karen, just stay in here and lock the door when I leave," I said it firmly so as to leave no room for debate, and I was out of the room before she said another word.

He's here. Bravo. He's going to rape my wife and make me watch.

It was quite dark, and my eyes quickly adjusted to what little light seeped in from the windows, even though the peripheral vision in my injured eye was compromised. I crept to the kitchen, opened the drawer, and grabbed a butcher knife. I prowled from room to room— spare bedroom, extra bathroom, hallway, dining room—at each corner and every doorway, poised to strike. *Slash-stab, slash-stab.* I knew someone was going to die—him or me.

When I got to the living room, I found it on the floor. It was a photograph of Karen and me from the wedding. Somehow, it had fallen off the wall. I checked the door and windows—all locked. My combatant was nowhere to be found.

I walked back down the hall and knocked on the door to the bedroom.

"Karen? It's me. It's okay. Let me in."

She did—and I told her everything. She didn't say much; she did say she was glad it was just a broken picture frame and that she'd clean it up in the morning. She then turned over to go back to sleep, and I laid down and tried to settle down. But I couldn't. My heart was surging; the room was buzzing. I tried to calm myself physically so as not to disturb Karen, but internally, I was freaking out!

If that were Bravo and he hadn't made a sound, he could've got in here and killed me—killed us—and I wouldn't have even known. I can't let that happen.

So the next day, while Karen was at work, I planted objects all over the house. Knives. A meat mallet. A baseball bat. If it could be used as a weapon, I hid it somewhere. I wasn't going to be left helpless if he ever showed up. A part of me was convinced he would. It was just a matter of when.

The nightmares started next. I had one each of the next two nights—both times, I woke up bathed in a cold sweat. The dreams were play-by-play reenactments of the abuse I suffered from Bravo. Everything happened in the dream exactly as it had in real life. The imagery was vivid, as though I was right back in the cell. I managed to get back to sleep both times, but my slumber was anything but restful. I woke often and tossed and turned. I took solace as I remembered where each weapon was stashed.

The next afternoon, officials from the prison stopped by to let me know I was going to need to attend therapy. They'd set up the first appointment for the following week to help me deal with the trauma from the hostage incident. Had they arrived a few days earlier, I would've poo-pooed the whole idea. But now? I didn't know what to expect, but I was certainly open to sitting down with a shrink. Somebody had to help me figure out what was going on.

That same night, I had another dream—but this one was different. I was back in the cell.

"This wasn't even for you, Houston!" Bravo was on the top bunk. He was laughing diabolically, the sound a hollow echo and eerily similar to Vincent Price in Michael Jackson's "Thriller" video. "But now you're here, so I guess I'm gonna have to kill you."

Bravo jumped down. He had a pillowcase in his hand.

"Houston? I'm hungry. I'm tired. And I'm getting ready to kill you."

He shoved the pillowcase over my head. I gasped. He immediately ripped it back off.

"No. I want you to see what I'm going to do to you."

He grabbed the long shank. It was silver and glimmering and had a cruciform hilt—King Arthur's Excalibur from lore, except that he was pointing it at me. Specifically, my chest.

Bravo placed his hand to his ear.

"Hmmm. I don't hear a *Voice*. Where's your precious *Voice*, Houston?" he screamed. "Where the *hell* is it now?"

He thrust the sword at me—into me—straight through my sternum, my esophagus, my spine. I tasted blood.

I woke up. It felt like I had just thumped down onto the mattress, dropped prone, and ramrod straight from ten feet up. I looked down at my chest, expecting to see the sword's hilt, the spray of blood. Nothing. Just me in my bed.

I wept. Quietly. I didn't want to wake Karen or have to respond when she asked me what I was crying about. I didn't want her to know. *I* didn't want to know.

Over the next ten days, I didn't go a single night without another twisted dream. Most of them ended in my death. Things started happening in the daytime as well. At the store that weekend, I was suddenly overcome with a sense of dread, like something didn't look right, didn't *feel* right. We were in the bread and cereal aisle, and it seemed to be closing in on me. Then a man tapped me on the shoulder.

I pivoted toward him, fists at the ready.

"Don't do that!" I yelled. "Why are you touching me?"

The man swiftly retreated. Karen looked equal parts embarrassed and scared out of her wits. Three days later, I went into a fast-food restaurant restroom. I locked the door behind me. As I stood at the urinal, I swore I could feel Bravo's blade against my testicles. My head jerked to the left, then to the right, convinced someone was behind me. It was impossible—I was all alone in the room. But my mind wouldn't accept reason.

Man, this is an ideal place to be taken hostage, I thought.

And so it went. Karen mostly kept quiet or to herself. I think she thought the less she said, the better off things would be. Besides, she was also pregnant, and dealing with that and with me at the same time was often overwhelming.

Every now and then, she'd say, "Donnie, you're overreacting," or "Baby, do you *really* think that's going to happen?"

She meant well, but I either responded in anger or not at all. She was frightened, confused, and her sense of security in me was being ripped away. She didn't know if what was happening to me was temporary or if this was just the way it was going to be.

Neither did I.

When I went to the first therapy appointment, it was unnerving and intimidating. I'd never been to a therapist before, and I was under the impression that if you did go to one, you must be crazy. The initial session was more of a consultation where he asked questions about my background, family, health, and similar surface items. I think he could tell I was a fish out of water and uncomfortable with the whole thing. I was set to see him twice each week, and it took me until the third week to calm my nerves enough to try to discuss what happened when I was taken hostage. Yet when I did, that was when things really started to get truly difficult.

I was experiencing a lot of trust issues then. I wasn't about to be upfront with anyone about anything. By week five, the sessions became so intense that I just couldn't hold it together. I was emotionally bound up. I'd cry and weep, and while my tears were ones of joy and gratitude for being alive, it still didn't seem to help me. I was an absolute mess, and there was one point I was even recommended to go into a psychiatric facility. They just didn't know what to do with me. But Karen wouldn't have any of that—she refused to let me be placed into an institution. I don't know if it was because she didn't think I needed it or that maybe she was in some form of denial about the situation. Perhaps she knew she didn't want to be alone when our baby was born. Either way, I wasn't put away, and the therapy continued. Ultimately, I was diagnosed with something called Post Traumatic Stress Disorder (PTSD), a condition that was still relatively new, at least under that name.

At home, things remained pretty stressful. Neither one of us knew how to deal with this—we were just too young. It didn't take much to get either one of us angry or upset at each other. I especially used to hate it when the night came because then I had to go to sleep. I tried everything I could to try to stay up, but eventually, the body succumbed—and then the nightmares resumed.

Many times, I didn't sleep because I was convinced Bravo was coming. I didn't want to be in a compromising position. I was on guard and in a high awareness state. I couldn't wait until the sun came up because then I knew it was over—at least for another twelve hours or so.

So here I was, living—maintaining—day by day, sometimes moment by moment. Even worse, I knew a huge challenge was looming, one that was going to put my months of therapy to the test and stretch my thinning sanity to the breaking point.

The time had come to face my biggest fear, to bring my darkest dreams to vivid life.

Bravo's day in court had arrived, and I had to be there.

CHAPTER 4

KAREN WANTED TO GO WITH ME, though only God knows why. I suppose she wanted to be there to support me, to try to see me through my days in court just like she was striving to see me through every other day.

But I told her, "No." My reasoning was simple, and I thought, exceedingly valid. I didn't want Bravo to see her, to know what she looked like so that he could send someone after her.

"If I happen to die," I told her, "I don't want anything to happen to you."

I'm sure those words weren't exactly a comfort to Karen, but she abided by my wishes. I'm so glad she did. Despite her amazing strength, I don't believe she could've handled what I saw when I first arrived. It would've freaked her out. I barely kept it together myself.

I'd never been to court before. Frankly, I hadn't even watched a TV show or movie with courtroom scenes. I was clueless, which explains why I showed up for the first day of the trial in sweatpants, gym shoes, and a t-shirt. Well, ignorance of proper courtroom etiquette wasn't the only reason for my attire. As far as I was concerned, I was showing up for a fight. I figured I had to dress ready for a brawl. That was my mentality.

I was prepped beforehand by the U.S. attorney for the type of questions I might face when on the stand, but I was not prepared for anything else I encountered. I was told to arrive at the prison, where I was then escorted via an underground tunnel to the court building. Upon arrival, I and everyone else going into the chamber went through a metal detector and were subjected to other security searches. When I walked into the courtroom itself, agents from the Bureau of Alcohol, Tobacco, Firearms, and Explosives lined the walls. It was intimidating and only served to feed the paranoia-driven fear that I already felt.

My PTSD was telling me that I was walking into a war zone. Looking around, I believed it.

I took a seat next to the United States attorney. "Calm down," she encouraged me, and I did the best I could.

Then Bravo was brought in. He was clean-shaven, minus the salt and pepper beard, and I hardly recognized him. Though he was totally nonchalant and didn't in any way acknowledge my presence there, I could feel my heart pounding. Though I had seen him almost every night in my dreams or living nightmares, this was the first time I'd actually seen him since I was taken hostage.

He won't hurt me this time, I told myself. *I'm ready for a fight.*

My inner bravado was offset by the six hours I spent that day on the witness stand. I had to talk in detail about all of the steps leading up to the incident, the particulars of how I ended up in the cell, and the specifics of what happened to me while I was held captive. I also had to respond to a bunch of false accusations—everything from being on Bravo's payroll to claims that I smuggled stuff into jail for him. It was grueling. The most difficult aspect of the testimony was reliving each interaction I had with Bravo in the cell. Though I had previously spoken of those things in therapy, it was another thing entirely to do it in a courtroom surrounded by men with automatic weapons and Bravo staring at me, often with a smirk on his face.

I could hear his mocking voice in my head.

I guess I'm gonna have to kill you. What are they gonna do to me anyway? Give me another life? I'm already serving two. What can they do to me?

When I was done testifying, I got down from the stand and, to my surprise, started walking straight toward Bravo. I have no idea what I looked like, but I know what I was thinking.

If I can just get to the man's throat, I can end this thing right now.

"He's not worth it, Donnie." It was the voice of the bailiff. "He's not worth it."

I kept walking.

"Please," the bailiff pleaded. "Let me do my job. I have to protect him. I know he's a slime ball, but I have to protect him."

Everybody around me stood up. I'm certain they thought we were getting ready to fight. The U.S. attorney gestured toward me.

"Just come over here, Donnie."

I still didn't stop—but I did turn right, away from where Bravo was still seated and toward my seat next to the attorney. I felt nauseous but hoped that I had at least intimidated him. I took my seat, inhaled a deep breath or two, and settled in for the duration.

The trial only lasted four days. I was there until the case was given over to the jury. I dressed appropriately for the remainder of the trial, and there were no more incidents, at least not in the courtroom.

At home, I was a wreck—I arrived home each day exhausted, physically and emotionally drained. My dreams intensified—I catnapped when I could but never slept for more than a couple of hours at a time. I felt violated, first as a hostage, then every day and night since then, and now once more through the rigors of the trial process.

I chose not to return to hear the verdict. I was confident he'd be found guilty, but I saw no point in me being there to hear it. Bravo received another 35 to 105 years for what he did to me, and I later learned he was indeed sent to the Alcatraz of the Rockies. But he lacked one thing when he got there. The badge of honor for killing a guard. After all, I was still alive.

And I was desperate to actually start living again.

~

The trial was over, and I knew I had to do something to stop Bravo from terrorizing my mind—and that was only going to happen as I overcame my PTSD. I didn't want to be the kind of guy where people felt sorry for me, or worse.

"Look at Donnie over there. That's why he's on drugs or on the corner out of his mind. It was because of what happened to him."

So I went to work to rehab myself. In addition to the therapy, the prison offered me a gym membership, so I took it, knowing that there was value in being physically healthy. The therapy continued as well, and it helped. But because I had grown up in church, not to mention my experience with the *Voice* during the hostage situation, I somehow sensed there was something more that I needed to change to experience full healing from my condition. I had no idea what that was, but I just knew God didn't get me out of that hostage situation alive for nothing.

Our baby was born on August 13, 1991. She was seven pounds, twelve ounces, healthy and beautiful. We named her Emery—and her presence was an added catalyst for me to become whole again as soon as I could. I wanted to be a father to her in every way a man should be a father to his daughter. I couldn't do that if my mind were besieged with fear. She was depending on me. Karen was depending on me. Failure was not an option.

At the gym, I met Mark. He was an older guy who had heard about my story on the news and befriended me as we worked out. We chatted at the gym. Afterward, he joined Karen and me for a bite to eat, and Mark gradually became something of a father figure to me.

He was also a Christian, and he and his wife Maria invited Karen and me to attend church with them. We did on a few occasions and had them over Sunday afternoon for dinner. While the ladies gabbed in the kitchen, Mark and I sat on the sofa and watched football–he'd always drop a nugget of wisdom on me about life or my marriage. He emphasized the importance of being an honorable man who takes care of and is patient with his wife. He really echoed the same principles my dad had taught me long ago, only this time I was listening. It's funny how boys can hear things from their fathers and not pay attention, then hear the same things from a friend later as an adult and see the value in the advice. He reinforced the need for me to be a good provider and love my wife sacrificially. He was never preachy or heavy-handed but told me these things in the course of regular conversation.

Mark and Maria were instrumental, along with another older couple named Margaret and George, who were our neighbors, in helping Karen and me to work on our relationship and navigate our way through the start of my recovery, and our early days as new parents. Margaret and George were ready babysitters for Emery, allowing Karen and I to go out every now and then. These couples were our angels.

Through Mark, I also started attending a weekly afternoon men's Bible study. I don't recall anything significant from the study itself, but it was the first time I really heard the Bible's teachings. I didn't intentionally apply anything particular to my situation with PTSD, but I could tell that what I learned comforted me.

I continued to progress, and Karen and I began drawing closer to one another. The vibe around the house was much better; it was a light time for us. Like any new parents, we were excited and nervous about raising Emery but embracing the newness of it all. As Christmas neared, we shopped for presents for her, put up the tree, and started forming our own family traditions.

The festive joy of the season was offset by the approach of December 17th and what had happened one year earlier on that date. It was a tough day and night. It was intense from a flashback perspective; I envisioned variations of what really happened, sometimes in dreamlike fashion and other times as though I was right back there in the cell. Self-condemnation also unexpectedly invaded my thinking. *Why would God save a no-good scoundrel like me?* I asked myself as I came out of one flashback sequence. *He probably should've let me be killed. It's not like I'm feeding the homeless or preaching revivals.* I made it through to the next day, though, and in the remaining days until Christmas, I fared well. I remained hyper-vigilant—even if my brain told me Bravo was buried and gone deep in a mountain in Colorado.

My brother, Ralph, and his girlfriend joined us for Christmas dinner, and this was when we started talking about leaving San Diego altogether to return to Michigan. We figured we could be around family and people older and wiser than us that could help us through any choppy waters to come. But the biggest reason behind the decision to move was money. As we started house shopping in California, we realized we could have a much larger home with a yard for less in Michigan than we'd pay for a slight upgrade from our current townhouse. Sure, I thought about the fact that being away from San Diego would also leave behind the place where I was taken hostage, but it wasn't as much of a factor in our decision as I thought it would be. In the end, we just wanted to go someplace with a better cost of living where Emery could grow and where we could meet all of her needs.

So, in the summer of 1992, we left it all behind—the Metropolitan Correctional Center in downtown San Diego, Bravo and the hostage ordeal and following trial, and even our new friends—to return to familiarity, comfort, and family. Our duo of angelic couples and other friends gave us a nice going-away party, and my therapist helped me connect with someone in Michigan who could continue my psychiatric care. Before we knew it, the tickets were purchased, the movers had come and gone, and we were on a plane bound for Detroit.

As I took my seat on the aisle next to Karen, it was like a chapter in life was closing for both of us. No matter what happened in the future, we knew we were never returning to California.

The aircraft reached cruising altitude, and I took a deep breath. It was going to be a fresh start. Better days were ahead. Emery was in my lap and looked about ready to go to sleep. I looked at Karen, smiled, and closed my eyes.

Karen said Emery slept most of the way.

As it turned out, so did I.

~

We stayed for a week in Detroit with Karen's sister and even looked at a couple of homes there before deciding to head across state to the Grand Rapids area. That first week, I was more relaxed, and my PTSD was lessened. It was weird, but I just knew I didn't have to worry about Bravo showing up in Detroit. *I'm on my turf now,* my mind told me. *I have home-field advantage.*

CHAPTER 5

MY LIFE'S EXPERIENCES and the ordeal I endured to get to where I am today have not been easy. I could say I had it worse, but there's always someone out there that's experienced more who could take the trophy from me. As humans living in an imperfect society, we always encounter problems. We may try our very best to avoid them, but more often than not, our best will not always be good enough, or perhaps it is how life was designed to be. The fact that we encounter problems in our journey through life isn't where the problem lies; it's how we react to these problems that life hurls our way that really matters. This is called the Pareto Principle (the 80-20 rule). This theory states that a large majority (typically 80%) of outcomes or effects are often driven by a few important causes (typically 20%).

This law can be applied in many ways. For example, for a businessperson, 80% of your customer's complaints/ recommendations, as the case may be, arise from how well or poorly your product meets their needs. As a church leader, 80% of the turnout you get or 80% of souls saved arise from how well or how often you do what is expected of you; teach, evangelize and pray. As a leader in an organization, 80% of the support and cooperation you get from your subordinates arises from how adept you are, especially in terms of your leadership skills. 80% of the success your favorite sports team enjoys is as a result of how hard they train. Life is 20% what happens to you and 80% how you react to it.

The 80-20 Rule is so simple yet so powerful. Understanding this rule is key to success as it saves you from getting bogged down in unnecessary and time-consuming detail. As I mentioned earlier, life happens to us all. However, a simple understanding of the Pareto Principle creates the disparity between those trapped in uncertainty/immobility and those who go on to pick the roses out from the thorns that surround them.

Now, what do you do differently? Skill up!

React to your problems the right way–This is the first and most important skill. See it however you wish, but life always gives you a choice. The excuse, "I had no choice," is just something we invented, in the long run, to exempt ourselves from blame and play the victim card (it's always easier to play the victim card). It is, however, important that we remind ourselves that by using that excuse to avoid what we need to do, there is always someone else avoiding that excuse and doing what we have failed to do. You should be responding instead with, "What is the way forward?"

Limiting beliefs: your ordeals do not make your contemporaries better than you. The fact that my partner, the other prison guard, escaped, and I got taken hostage did not mean I was incapable. I would have done myself more harm than good if I had focused on that and held on to the past and let the fear or even the PTSD limit me. It was just unfortunate that that happened to me. Just as it was me in there, it could have been anyone else. There was really nothing I did to deserve what happened, and I had to come to an understanding of that if I were to continue on with a happy life.

The Importance of Mindset: Take total control of your mind, set good standards for yourself, rid your mind of doubt and overcome your fears, build your confidence and self-esteem, see yourself the way some others may never see you, and what's more, never stop dreaming. I learned that I could not play "victim" forever. I intentionally began to live beyond all that happened and was able to recapture many of the plans I had for my life before the incident.

I took the initiative. I took deliberate actions. I went back to school to improve my skill sets so I could, at the very least, give myself a chance in this ever-changing economy. I realized that in life, we never stop getting better, and your content has to align with the goals you have set for your life. You control your own destiny, so make the best use of your time, and integrate the 80-20 rule if you can.

CHAPTER 6

NOW, WHILE READING THIS BOOK, you might be thinking, "It is always easier said than done." No doubt this is true, "doing" usually takes a lot of effort, discipline, determination, and sacrifice. But can it be done? A million times, yes! However, before you can effectively take the lead and go where you need to get to, there are important things you must note. These principles helped me on my path to rebuilding my life. These were the challenges that lay before me:

- The challenges of leadership
- Internal versus external leadership
- The indispensability of skill and knowledge in every field of life and the ability of these skills to sometimes skyrocket you to places you just are not ready for yet.
- Displaced from job, middle-aged man starting over with no formal education.
- External vs. Internal Conflicts in Leadership

External Conflict

External conflict arises within yourself and others, possibly among those placed under you, or the client you are serving, or the members of your church, or even as a team captain or coach supervising the other members of the team. Not everyone will be okay with you being in the position you are in. Some may feel the need for you to prove your worth. Others may think you are not the best fit for the job or that they could do it better themselves. In the long run, you may find yourself in a struggle to please clients who expect your services and products to be better than what they have already experienced from your competitors in business, and you would be wrong to let any of that deter you. Believe in your abilities and what you can do, and do your very best with the help of God.

Leaders are not afraid of becoming a target for gossip, criticism, or scrutiny. Yes, these things do happen; criticism and obstacles will come from all different angles, but you will survive it. True leaders learn from adversity. As a true trailblazer, hardships are inevitable but remember that you are making the path clear for others coming after you.

Internal Conflict

This is the conflict that goes on within one's self. What's called the imposter syndrome is usually a characteristic of this type of conflict. The impostor syndrome (also known as impostor phenomenon, fraud syndrome, or the impostor experience) is a psychological pattern in which an individual doubts his/her accomplishments or skills. It is characterized by a persistent internalized fear of being exposed as a "fraud" or "imposter."

I did not think myself good enough or deserving. I felt unqualified, like I was not ready to move on from what I used to be to what I could be. This feeling is very common, especially among perfectionists, geniuses, or individuals, like me, who have been through some terrible past experience. Even achieving the highest levels of education and advanced degrees does not satisfy this type of person. The best strategy to overcome this syndrome is to acknowledge the thoughts associated with it and to put those thoughts in perspective. Identify the thoughts and do not engage them. Do not make the mistake of trying to analyze and think them through. Dwelling on such thoughts will keep you drowning in the pool of impossibilities.

Know this also, leadership doesn't start in the executive office. Leadership begins in the foundational positions of a business: the company mailroom, the entry-level position or pews of the church, a team's bench player. So make the most of whatever position you are placed in at the moment. In those positions, you build relevant skills and core values, empathy, versatility, and tenacity. You learn by working your way up the leadership ladder.

Your skillset and education will often take you places that your mind did not believe you could go or that you feel you are not ready to handle just yet. More often than not, these thoughts are just in your head, and frequently you learn best in the line of duty. Do not be afraid to take up challenging roles; they make you better and stronger.

Put in your best effort, and try to make it work, do not fear the worst at the very start.

Don't just settle for the "status quo" or "fitting in" and then, in the long run, lose sight of what's important. Get out of your comfort zone and go for what you want. You never know what possibilities lie ahead until you try.

The Importance of Mentorship/Relationships

Mentorship and relationships are vital to growth in so many ways. It is said that no man is an island—man is naturally an interdependent being. Mentors serve as the expert force steering you in the right direction in the journey of self-discovery and development. These mentors have had more experience with life, have made their mistakes, and have excelled through the worst odds. Relationships strengthen your will to excel through difficult times. They are made up of the individuals who are always there, cheering you on in the darkest points of your life. As I struggled with the effects of my ordeal, the people I had around me gave me the strength to keep pushing, to want to try that much more, even if it strained me. The thought that I had a wife who needed me to be alright gave me the courage to suppress the voices in my head, trying to push me to fail.

Don't Just Survive, Thrive!

Sustainability - How to thrive and not just survive in this new "NORM" in the business world. As a person of influence or as a leader, learn to grow and adapt to change. Be open to new and innovative ideas and suggestions; be accommodating in the toughest of conditions; be limitless.

The lessons learned at the lowest points in your life are lessons you should hold onto most dearly. Every experience, good or bad, is a valuable lesson. Learn from those lessons along the way and keep growing.

No Challenge=No Growth - We grow best through our experiences. For some, challenges successfully propel them beyond their perceived "limit."

Adaptability - Even with a change of environment, job or circumstance, I learned to adapt and adjust to the changes I faced. The environment was new: the people, the norms, the standards, and living conditions, so also were the expectations.

Gratitude

Gratitude is an all-encompassing factor. Be grateful for the very little things, for what you have, your experiences, and the people you encounter along your journey. More so, as a leader, show gratitude. Human resource is the greatest of all forms of resource; it cannot be stated more clearly. A little appreciation goes a long way in getting the best out of an individual. Here's an easy way to show the progression of what I'm talking about.

Gratitude> increased happiness>
motivation/drive> achieved goals> success.

CHAPTER 7

The People, Product, Processes, Profit, Passion, Purpose Concept

I STARTED MY PROFESSIONAL CAREER in education and quickly climbed the ranks from classroom teacher to assistant principal, to principal, and finally executive director/superintendent. My ability to transform schools and increase student achievement earned me a reputation as a change agent and a reformer. Leading some of the most challenging schools and students to realize their best and highest use became my life's work for nearly 20 years. Today, I serve as an executive in the senior housing industry, managing 60 plus employees and a $7 million budget.

Becoming successful was not easy for me, but I was determined to live a better life and make a name for myself even after everything I had been through. I felt so discouraged by the events of my past, always screaming negative thoughts in my head. But I really wanted to make things right and try to make up for all the time I lost to my ordeal. I relied on the following principles to guide me on my journey from ordinary to extraordinary:

PEOPLE

It really all starts with people and relationships. The very root of success, whether economically or personally, stems from people and your networks. The network of people around you is a great indication of how far you have come and how far you can go. I really believe that I could not have battled through my issues without the love and support of the people in my life.

So how can the people around you help you gain sustainable success? Think of your network of people like options available to a task or goal. It is almost like multiple connections to one source; the source is the goal, and the people are the connections that you have, so you are almost always connected, even if one connection may be down. People are the driving force to your destination—they will help get you to where you want to be.

The place and priority of people in your life are very important. Other than those closest to you who you rely on for emotional support, surround yourself with leaders. Surround yourself with people who have already achieved the things that you want in your life. Winners want to be around other winners. This does take a level of emotional intelligence. The application of emotional intelligence will help you win peoples' trust, which is paramount to sustainable success as a leader.

At the beginning of my professional career in education, teamwork was my greatest ally and strength. Being able to positively collaborate and work with people provides support and helps you achieve whatever your leadership goals might be. Every successful leader has mastered the art of successful relationship building with the people he/she is leading.

This can also make a huge impact or change the lives of the people you lead. People respond to you more when they can see just how much you value them. As a leader, you should identify and encourage the best in people. Help them grow; help them become the best versions of themselves.

PRODUCTS

Every successful business has a product or service they provide. Every product or service has a purpose. It's key to understand in whatever business you are in that the uniqueness of a product or service can set it apart from the competition. It's important to remember that customers buy products or use services to meet a need or solve a problem. Consciously or unconsciously, your customer or client will always be asking, "What's in it for me?" Your product or service has to deliver solutions and satisfy needs, or you will not be successful.

PROCESSES

Processes are fundamental to an organization's culture. They define how things are done and why they're done that way. Business leaders are under immense pressure to remain competitive, decrease costs, and increase productivity by improving business processes. And because organizations are constantly changing as they respond to internal and external pressures, continual process improvement can strengthen leadership and team effectiveness and lead to growth.

Growth does not occur without effective strategy execution. However, effective strategy execution is one of the biggest challenges facing business leaders today. Traditionally one of the biggest hurdles is that employees tend to be resistant to change. And herein lies the problem. The people expected to carry out the processes had nothing to do with developing those processes, and they aren't invested in implementing them. So how do you prevent the new procedures from being tossed aside?

The key is to make all business processes part of your organization's day to day conversation at all levels. The hope is to foster an environment of continual improvement, one where processes and their outcomes can be tracked and regularly reviewed and updated. Process improvement is an ongoing endeavor that needs to grow and change along with your organization and its people.

PROFIT

The next step is profits. I think it's easy to assume that successful leadership likely leads to increased profits. But the opposite is usually true as well. Poor leadership can directly affect a business's bottom line. In a 2015 Forbes Magazine article, the author actually put this good-bad leadership formula to the test. They studied reports of more than 50,000 managers and were able to show the relative effectiveness or ineffectiveness of those leaders with respect to their companies bottom line.

In a nutshell, the study showed quite clearly that poor leaders lost money, good leaders made a profit, and extraordinary leaders (the top 10%) made money and more than doubled the company's profits compared to the other two groups combined. Developing leaders who inspire people to perform at a higher level will directly affect productivity and profits. Good leaders create more economic value than poor leaders, and extraordinary leaders create far more value than good ones.

PASSION

How do you characterize success? Most people believe that success can only be reached the moment you get to your final destination and can only be measured in dollar signs. There is probably some truth to that, but I think it's important not to lose respect for the journey it took to get you to where you are going or where you are now. I think if you asked most successful businesspeople how they were able to make things work, they would probably list off a number of tangible steps to their success, but the foundation is more likely found in their passion for what they are doing. During my journey through my career, business, and leadership, what has kept me going was passion!

There have been times in my life where I felt lost. My experience in the prison stole much of my self-confidence and had me living in fear. But the moment I found purpose and began to pursue that purpose, I began to see progress in my life, and my passion suddenly burned once more like wildfire. The greatest feeling any leader could have is the feeling of steady and sustainable progress.

The most important part of sustaining success as a leader in a business venture, church, or any other field is passion. Managing a business and all that goes with it can be extremely draining and all-consuming. Passion, especially during the toughest times, will carry you through and keep you focused on your goals.

Do you enjoy what you are doing? Or do you get tired whenever you think about doing it? Passion is not just all about the success or being the fuel to keep going; it is also about what you love doing. As a leader, how can you expect the people around you to excel and care if you don't set the example for them? All my successes as a leader can be attributed to getting the best out of people, building a passion platform for others to stand on. Make sure you love what you are doing; it is the only thing that can get you through the challenges that will come. The tough times will test your resolve, but you will get through it. Be passionate about being a leader, and it will pave your way to sustainable success!

PURPOSE

And finally, purpose. Building on the same foundation as passion, purpose is an essential piece to the business leadership puzzle. It can be manifested in the simplest of things, like getting to work a little early to set that example for others. I have realized that every action I take gets me closer to or farther away from my success. Establishing this sense of purpose provides guidance. Each morning, I remind myself of why I began my business in the first place and what was expected of my business, and in the course of the day, I work towards that.

When it comes to a company's sense of purpose, more than ever, it is being affected by the changing world around us. The population at large is becoming more highly attuned to companies' moral compasses. Studies have shown that nearly three-quarters of adults who were polled agreed that public companies should be mission-driven as well as committed to customers and shareholders.

The concept of meaningful work is hardly new. I think for most people feeling connected to a broader sense of meaning through our work is a core part of what makes it enjoyable for us as human beings. It's more important than ever for leaders to make a stronger effort to connect people to a sense of purpose at work. The challenge is being authentic with that sense of purpose. It's not an easy task, but with the right mindset and with the guidance of these principles I have put in front of you, belief can be manifested into reality.

I hope this has struck a chord with you. My wish is that my story and my life can be an example of what can be accomplished with a little work and a lot of "want to."

> "A genuine leader is not a searcher for consensus
> but a molder of consensus."
>
> ~ *Martin Luther King Jr.*

THANK YOU FOR READING MY BOOK!

DOWNLOAD YOUR FREE GIFTS

Read This First

Just to say thanks for buying and reading my book, I would like to give you a 100% bonus gift for FREE, no strings attached!

To Download Now, Visit:
www.DonnieHoustonSpeaks.com/Freegift

I appreciate your interest in my book, and I value your feedback as it helps me improve future versions of this book. I would appreciate it if you could leave your invaluable review on Amazon.com with your feedback. Thank you!

Made in the USA
Columbia, SC
03 August 2021